THE MAGICAL MII
GARDEN FRIENDS

Black Background Coloring Book
for Adults and Teens

MW01463643

Copyright © 2025 by The Roaring Reader

The Roaring Reader

CONTENTS:

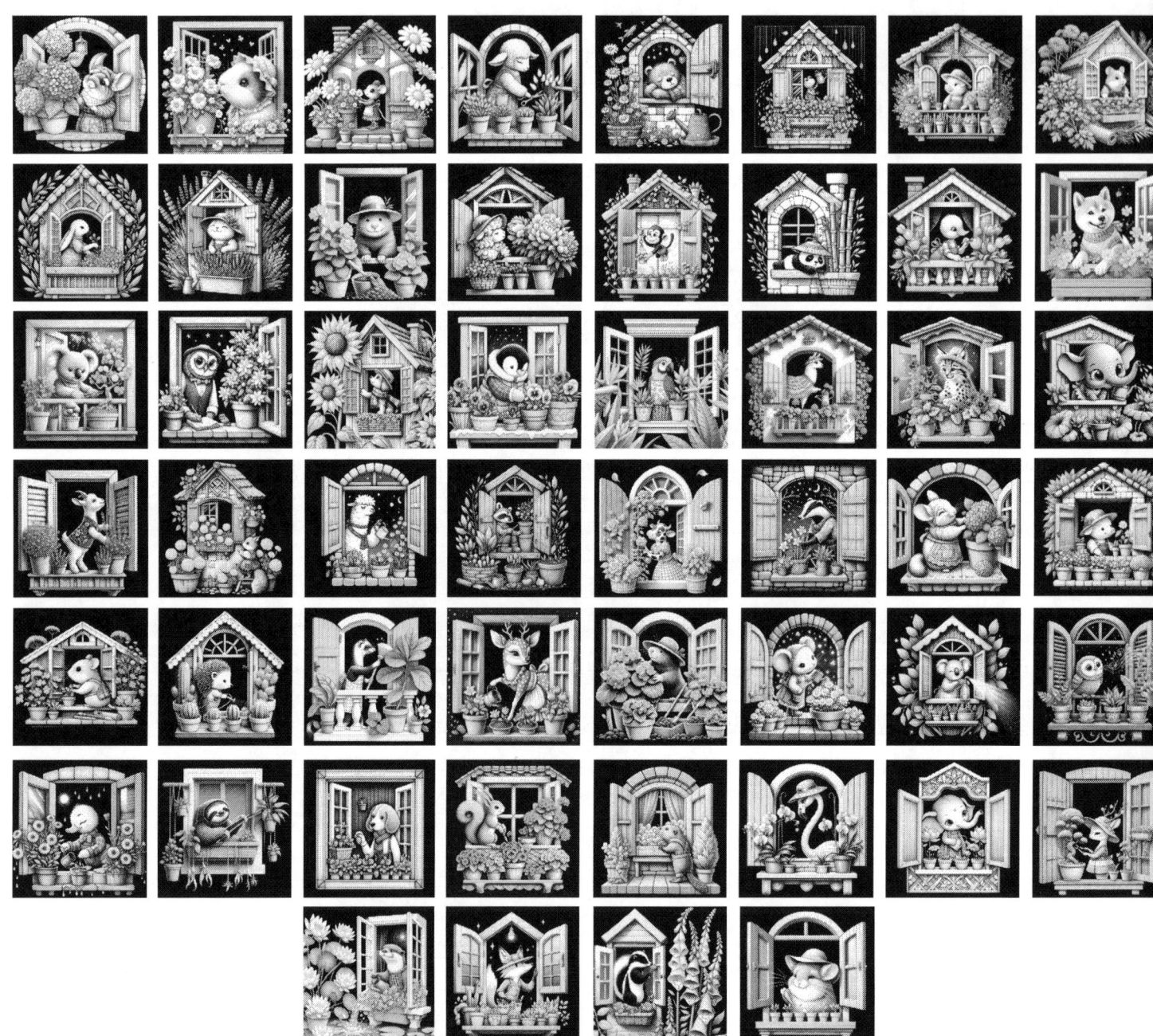

THIS BOOK BELONGS TO:

....

Discover More Unique Creations by The Roaring Reader!
Stay connected for updates on our latest books:

🌐 Website: www.roaringcolors.com

 ⬛ Facebook: fb.com/theroaringreader

⬛ Instagram: @theroaringreader

📲 Scan the QR code to explore now!

TEST YOUR COLORS:

Thank You!

I want to sincerely thank you for choosing my coloring book. Your support means the world to me, and I hope you've enjoyed coloring as much as I enjoyed creating these designs.

If you enjoyed the book, I would be incredibly grateful if you could leave a positive review to share your thoughts. Your feedback helps others discover my work and inspires me to create even more.

However, if for any reason you're not fully satisfied or have any concerns, please don't hesitate to contact me directly before leaving a review. I'm committed to ensuring that you have a positive experience and would be happy to resolve any issues. You can reach me via email at theroaringcolors@gmail.com or through my Facebook page at The Roaring Reader: https://www.facebook.com/theroaringreadercoloring/

Thank you again for your support, and happy coloring!

Warm regards,
The Roaring Reader

The Roaring Reader

Made in the USA
Middletown, DE
29 April 2025

74899250R00062